JOURNALS FOR EVERYONE

Journals For Everyone
ISBN 10– 1986587355
ISBN 13 - 978-1986587358